The Chinese Word for Horse and Other Stories

by John Lewis · illustrated by Peter Rigby

Schocken Books · New York

First published by Schocken Books 1980
First printing

Copyright © stories John Lewis 1976, 1977, 1978
Copyright © illustrations and design Peter Rigby 1976, 1977, 1978

Library of Congress Cataloging in Publication Data

Lewis, John.
   The Chinese word for horse and other stories.

   CONTENTS: The Chinese word for horse. – The Chinese
man and the Chinese woman. – The Chinese word for thief.
   1. Chinese language – Etymology – Anecdotes, facetiae,
satire, etc. 2. Calligraphy, Chinese – Anecdotes, facetiae, satire, etc.
I. Rigby, Peter. II. Title.
PZ4.L67417Ch 1980 [PR6062.E943] 495.1'81 79-25679

Manufactured in the United States of America

When you read these Stories...

...characters lettered in red – like the one on this page
are actual Chinese words as the Chinese would write them.
If you miss any of the meanings of the words as you read each
story, they are all given again at the end of the story.

The Chinese Word for Horse

If you want to understand this story,
you have to learn some Chinese words.
What does this word look like?
A horse of course.

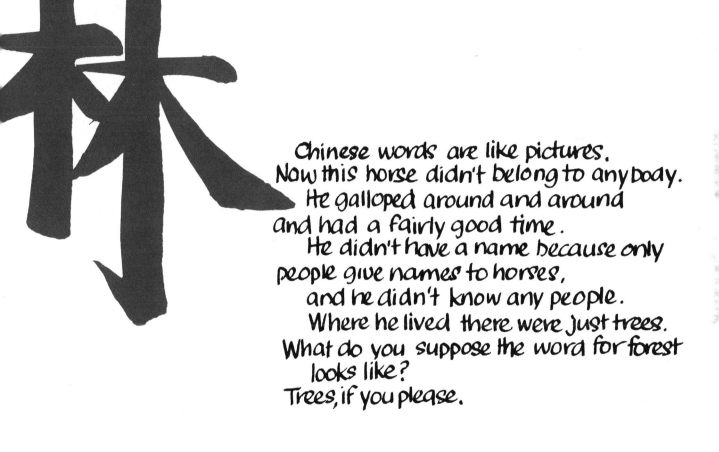

Chinese words are like pictures.
Now this horse didn't belong to anybody.
　　He galloped around and around
and had a fairly good time.
　　He didn't have a name because only
people give names to horses,
　　and he didn't know any people.
　　Where he lived there were just trees.
What do you suppose the word for forest
　　looks like?
Trees, if you please.

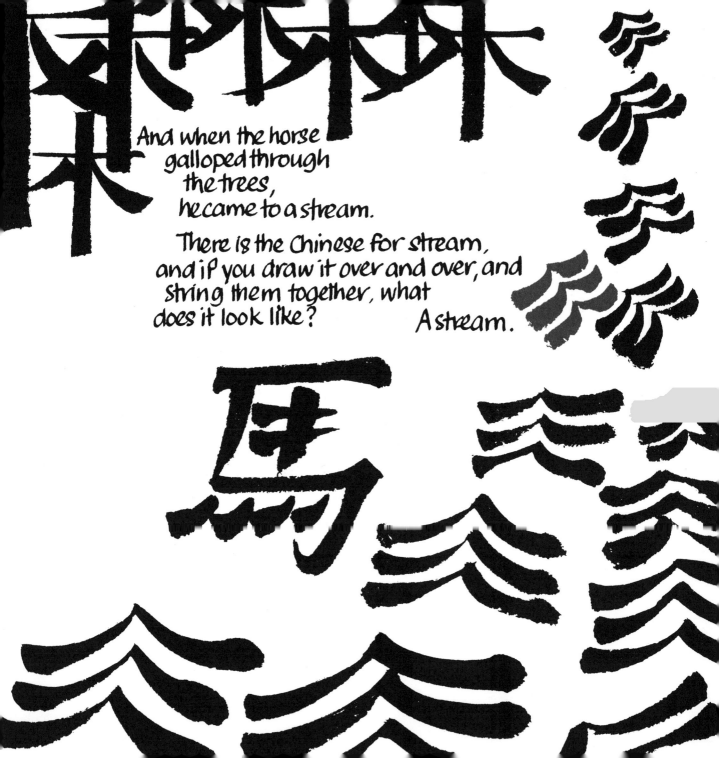

And when the horse
galloped through
the trees,
he came to a stream.

There is the Chinese for stream,
and if you draw it over and over, and
string them together, what
does it look like?

A stream.

The horse never crossed the stream
because it was a bit tricky, and he was
    quite happy galloping around in the trees.
One day he was galloping along and
    suddenly came to a stop - he had
heard a noise.

Creak, creak, creak.
What on earth is that, he thought.
    And he went straight away and looked
between the trees across the stream.
    On the other side he saw a man coming
along pulling a cart with a wheel that
    squeaked. It needed a drop of oil.

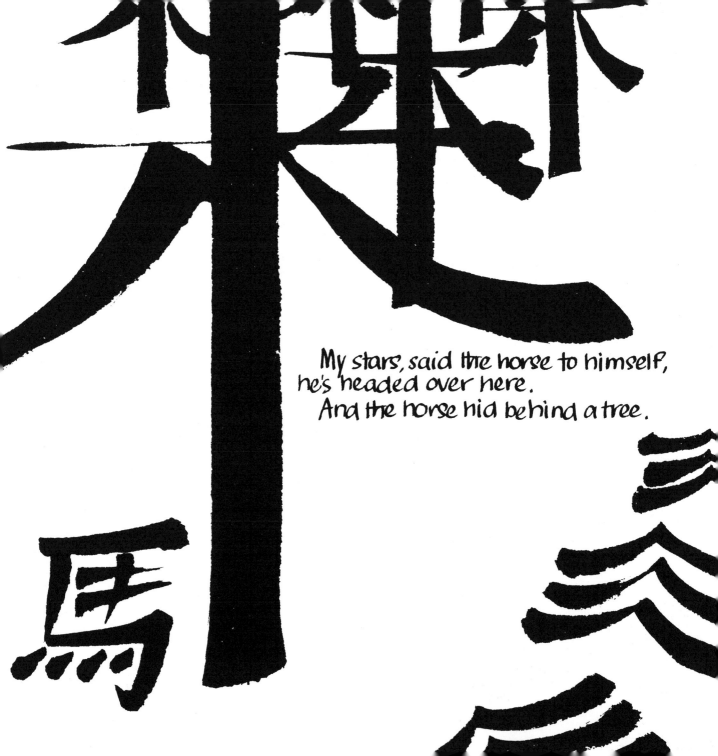

My stars, said the horse to himself,
he's headed over here.
And the horse hid behind a tree.

人車

The man stopped his cart at the stream.
He stood and had a think.
   He wanted to start a farm.
He thought, if I go over there on the other
   side of the stream, I'll have to clear
away all those trees.
   If I stay here, the ground is clear already.
And that stream looks a bit tricky.

He looked up into the sky and saw clouds.
Rain began to fall from the clouds.
    He said to himself, if I have my fields
under that rain, things ought to grow.

    All that season the man worked hard.
There was plenty of rain and things
    began to grow.
From the other side of the stream, the
    horse still galloped around and around
among the trees, but now he had
    something new to interest him

    He often came to the edge of the stream
to watch the man work his fields.
    After a while, he stopped hiding behind
a tree when he came to watch.

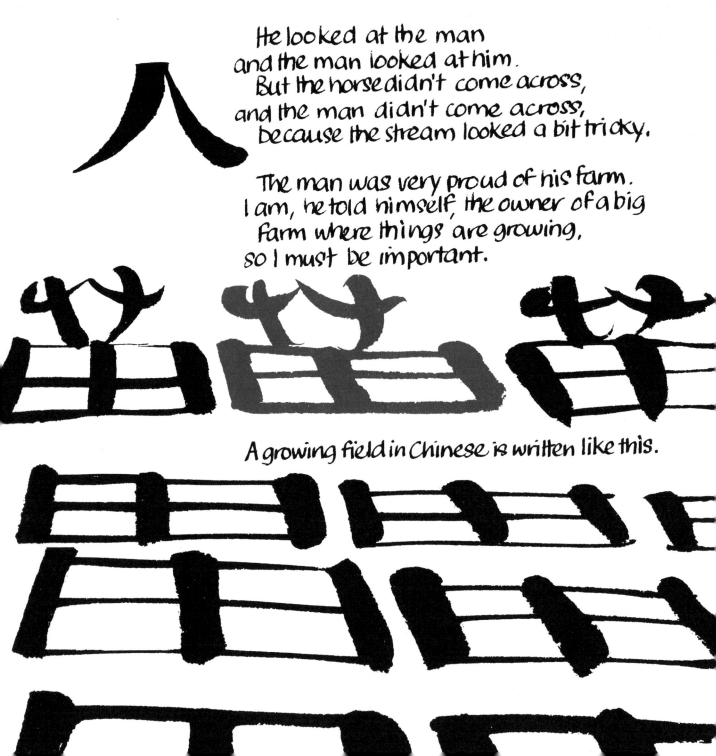

He looked at the man
and the man looked at him.
But the horse didn't come across,
and the man didn't come across,
because the stream looked a bit tricky.

The man was very proud of his farm.
I am, he told himself, the owner of a big
farm where things are growing,
so I must be important.

A growing field in Chinese is written like this.

And he changed from an
ordinary man into the Chinese
word for a gentleman
and a knight.
The horse noticed that he
looked taller, with his head
in the clouds, and didn't
work as hard in the fields.

One day when the horse
was galloping around
among the trees, having a
fairly good time he thought
he heard a noise.

Swish! Swish! Swish! swish!

The horse came to the edge
of the stream to see what it could be.

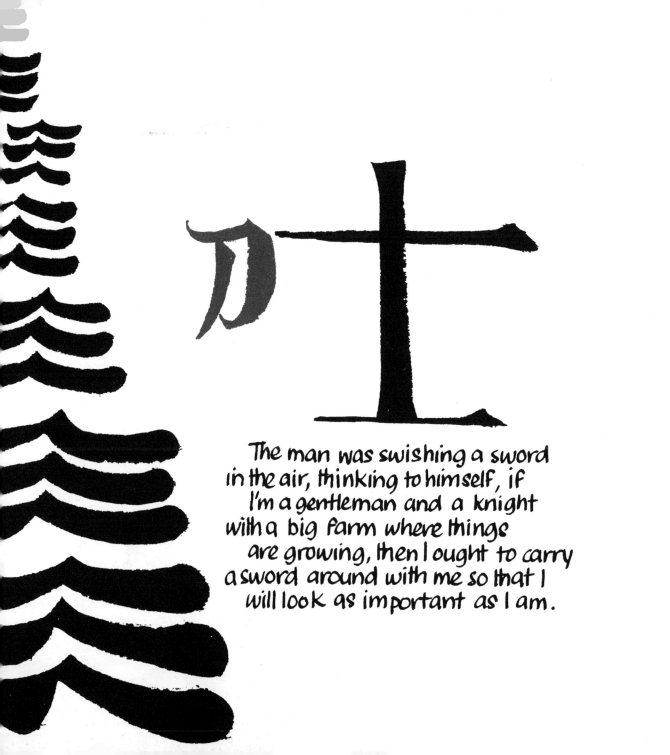

The man was swishing a sword
in the air, thinking to himself, if
I'm a gentleman and a knight
with a big farm where things
are growing, then I ought to carry
a sword around with me so that I
will look as important as I am.

The horse was a bit frightened by
the sound of the sword swishing in the air.
He decided he would go back to
hiding behind a tree while he watched.
Though it sounded dangerous,
the horse saw that the man looked
important swishing his sword.

He kept on hiding as he watched,
but nevertheless, he began to enjoy
watching.

The horse swished his tail admiringly,
while the man swished his sword.
The man heard the horse's tail and
said what a beautiful echo.

Days passed, and the man was
so happy swishing his sword that
he didn't take heed of the
change in the weather.

It wasn't raining so much.
Then it stopped altogether.
  Things stopped growing.
The horse wondered why the man
  didn't dip a bucket in the
stream to water his fields.
  But the man was too busy
swishing his
  sword.

Things not only stopped growing,
they began to wither.
    The fields dried up.
And, because there was nothing
    to eat in the fields, the man
felt hungry.
    He looked silly pretending
to be a gentleman and a knight
    with a sword, when things weren't
growing, and he didn't have a farm-
    that you could call a farm- anymore.

He went to the stream to get water
for his fields, but the stream was dry.
    If I don't get something to eat,
he thought, I'll die.
    Wait a minute, he said to himself,
I have a sword.
    I'll hunt for that horse and eat him.
This stream used to be a bit tricky
 to cross, before, now that it's dry
I can walk right over.

Watching from behind his tree,
the horse, of course, could see what
was in the man's mind.
He didn't like the look of it,
and he galloped away, around
and around, among the trees.

Unfortunately for that horse,
said the man, a man is cleverer
at hunting than a horse is.
That horse, he said, keeps galloping
around and around because
he thinks that I am running
around and around after him,
So I will wait behind this tree
until he comes around again.

And that is exactly what the man did.
The horse came galloping around again
   and the man sprang out at him,
swishing his sword.
   The horse cried out, wait! don't kill me...
The man said, why shouln't I ?
   I must kill you or I will starve to death.

The horse begged him not to be hasty:
when you've eaten me you'll have
no more to eat and you'll be no better off.
Instead, I have a plan that can save you.

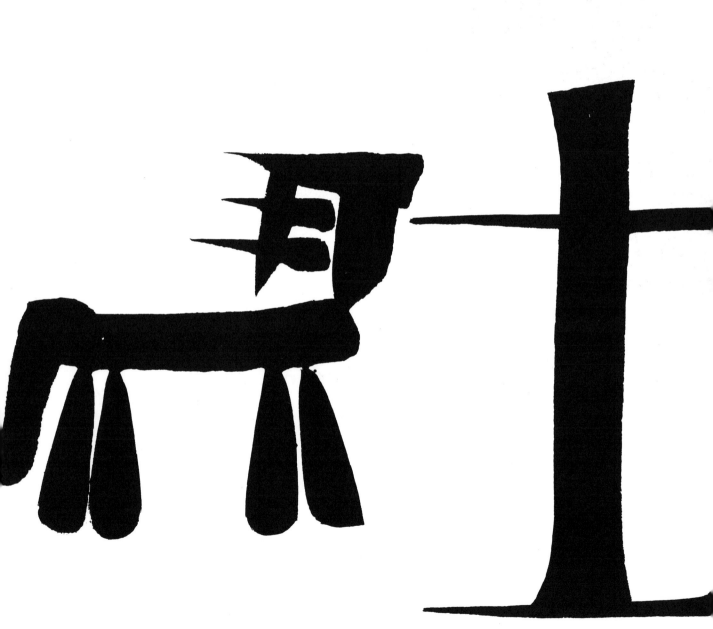

The man held his sword and listened.
The horse told him, the rain will come
   again soon, and things will grow again.
Enough things will survive to see you
   through till next season.
But if you really want to be a gentleman
   and a knight with a sword,
you must have bigger crops than that.
   You must dam the stream and make
a lake when the rain comes again,
   so that you will always have water.

Ha! said the man, how can I work
   in the fields and build a dam,
and still have time left over to
   be a gentleman and a knight
with a sword?

The horse began to tell him how,
and luckily, while he was explaining,
it started to rain and the man
decided to go along with the horse's idea.

While the horse was still telling it,
they both crossed over to the man's farm
before the new rain could fill the stream.
The man soon discovered the truth
of what the horse had said.

When he had a horse to pull
the cart, he could carry the earth
to build a dam.
When he had a horse to pull the plough,
he could farm more fields.
And when he had a horse to carry
water from the dam when the rain
stopped falling, he could grow
more things and have a bigger farm,
and still have time to be a gentleman
and a knight and swish his sword.

My word, he even had a horse to ride on.
You see what this story means –
a little horse sense and you're
a lot better off.

When the horse belonged to the man,
what name do you suppose he gave him?

There were no other horses to tell him
apart from, so the man
simply called him - Horse.

Horse

Forest

Man

Cart

Stream

Rain cloud

Gentleman

Sword

Growing field

The Chinese Man and the Chinese Woman

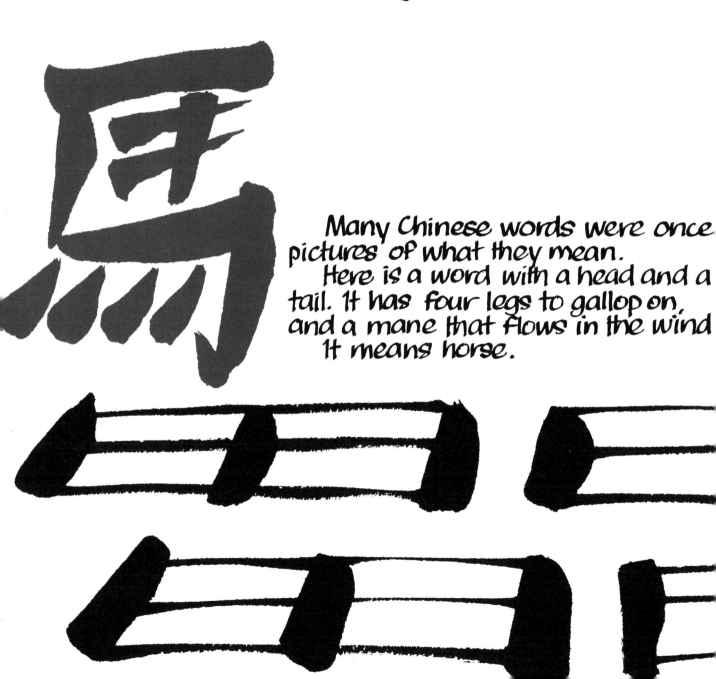

Many Chinese words were once pictures of what they mean.
Here is a word with a head and a tail. It has four legs to gallop on, and a mane that flows in the wind. It means horse.

This particular horse used to have a fairly good time simply galloping around and around in the fields.

A square divided into four is the Chinese for fields. Fields with sprouts are growing fields.

馬夫刀

The fields stretched almost to the eastern horizon where you can see the sun rise on clear blue days.

The fields and the horse belonged to a farmer who wore in his hair the Chinese pin that marks a man's coming of age.

Although the horse had a fairly good time galloping around by himself, he enjoyed it much more with the man on his back swishing his sword.

The man would swish his sword
on the one side and then on the other,
shouting: "Haw!" or "Yaw!" or "Yaw haw!"
They did this day after day till they
got tired of it.

The man said to the horse,
"It may be amusing to a horse to go
galloping around and around day after
day, but it's not much of a life for
a man of property."

The horse didn't say a word.

This man became very unhappy.
"Look at all my fields," he said.
The horse looked at his fields.
"Look at my horse."

The horse looked over his shoulder
at himself and swished his tail.
"Look how proudly I stand and
carry my sword.
I have all this, and yet I need
something more."

Just to be friendly, the horse said,
" You have a cart as well.

"What good is an old creaking cart?" the man complained. "Do I have so little to be proud of, that I have to be proud of a cart? A cart is for a simple farmer, not for a gentleman. I need something else."

"You have a shed," the horse added quietly.

"A shed!" the man shouted. "A shed is just a roof to put over a cart." And that is what the Chinese word for shed looks like.

The man sat himself down on a stool and gazed into the trees beyond his fields.

The morning song of birds seemed to give a voice to every branch. You can see three open mouths of birds in the trees in the Chinese word for birdsong.

How can you listen to birds singing and not be happy?

"Why am I unhappy?" he asked.

Around him flowers were opening
to the sun. How can you sit among flowers
and not be happy?

"Why am I unhappy?" he asked again.

The horse said, "If you want to know why
you are unhappy, you will have to go and
find a man who is happy, and ask him
what makes him happy."

The farmer sighed and climbed on the
horse saying. "I should have known that
a horse couldn't have the right answer.

日

The Chinese word for gate looks like a gate.
They rode out through the gate into the world.
    They found a man who had only a few
fields, and yet the man was happy. Beside
him was the woman that you can see in this
Chinese word. The man's wife was helping
him in the fields. They were both happy.

    "Good morning," the horseman said,
"What makes you such a happy man?"
    The man said, "I don't know. When you are
happy you never ask yourself why."

    They rode on. Now and then the knight
swished his sword, but he got no pleasure
out of it. He said, "Haw! Yaw!" and "Yaw! Haw!"
several times, but his heart wasn't in it.

They came to a second man resting
in the shade of a tree. He had a happy smile
on his face.

"Why the happy smile?" asked the rider.
"I'm simply happy," the man said, "I've no
idea why, but my wife is happy, too, perhaps
she can tell you."
They turned and asked the wife.

She said modestly, "My husband can
answer any question better than I can.
Whatever I want to know, I ask him."

So they rode on. Clouds cut out the warmth of the sun. A cold, heavy rain began to fall. The man was more unhappy than ever.

He said, "Haw!" and began to take out his sword. Then he put it back again. They sheltered under some trees.

The horse saw how unhappy his master was and he made a suggestion, " Each of these men had a wife - perhaps they are happy because they have wives to keep them company."

The man pooh-poohed the idea,
"If company were all 1 needed, 1
would be happy because 1 have a horse.
Let's ride on - the rain is letting up."

They met a third man. He, too, had
a wife. He was a happy man, as well.
"Can you tell me," asked the horseman
again, "What makes you happy?"

"1 cannot tell you," said the man,
"1'm only a poor farmer. 1 have no horse,
1'm not a swordsman. Your sword would
look clumsy in my hands - 1 suppose
1 am just easily contented."

The rider was thoughtful as they rode on.
Then he said to the horse, "It may be that,
because you are only a horse and cannot
be as wise as a man, you looked for a
simple answer and found the truth.
    Now I, being wiser, was looking for
an answer that needed a lot of thinking
about."
    The horse listened carefully,

The man continued, "There may be
something in the answer you have stumbled
on: all these men had wives and all these
men were happy."

The horse said, "Look, there's a young
woman in that field. She doesn't appear to
have a husband."

"I can see what you're thinking," the
man said, "if I ask the young woman to
be my wife then I, too, will be happy? Is
that so? Again, I must remind you that
a man is wiser than a horse. Look at that
young woman - have you ever seen
anyone so unhappy. All the men we met
had happy wives. We must ride on."

Further on they heard singing. It was beautiful singing. They followed the sound of the singing until they came upon another young woman happily working by herself.

The man smiled knowingly at the horse, "You see, he said, that is the kind of woman to make a man happy."

The man went without delay and asked the young woman to marry him.

"Marry you?" she said, "I've already promised myself to another man."

He put his head between his hands.
"The only woman I can find who doesn't
seem to be married is an unhappy woman."

"I was unhappy yesterday," the woman
said, "but then a man asked me to marry him."

The horse looked at the man. The man looked at the horse. Then he leapt onto the horse and rode off swishing his sword, shouting, "Haw!"

They returned at full gallop till
they came near where the unhappy
woman worked in the fields alone.
     When they could see her the man
reined in his horse and walked
quietly over to the woman.

大女

The man stood in front of the
woman. She looked up. He said,
"I have come to ask you to be my wife."

The young woman looked at him in surprise. Then she looked down at the ground. The man had to kneel to see her face.

And when he looked at her face, he saw that she was smiling.

He carried her away on the horse
to his many fields and they were married
and lived happily.

The horse riding swordsman took great pride in being a husband. He was still proud to swish his sword. He was proud of his horse and his fields. He was even proud of his old cart shed.
And he was happy.

And that is why the Chinese word for contentment is a roof with a woman under it.

Now you know nine more Chinese words. If all the stories of the Knight and the Horse were told you would know dozens.

Man

Woman

Contentment

Sunrise

Gate

Stool

Flower

Shed

Birdsong

The Chinese Word for Thief

It was the time when only firewood is harvested.
The farmer and his wife were glad to be under
the shelter of their roof.

Here is the Chinese word for roof. And look
at the word for fire - no one who could stay by
his fire went out of the house.

The wife watched her porridge pot and worried
to see so little in it; hunting was poor and all they
had to eat came from winter stores.
But when the winter is hard, everyone will
make do with a smaller share - except a thief.

The Chinese word for thrift is a picture of a
storehouse. It has a roof with bundles of grain
hanging under it, and double walls.
The farmer's storehouse stood by a river, a
flowing line for the mid current with ripples
along the banks.

And wherever the river has frozen over, the Chinese add two sharp lines of frost that make a picture of a snowflake which is their way of writing ice.

If the man and his wife were worried indoors by the fire, outdoors in the cold, their horse was very worried indeed. Not the least of his worries was the unsafe footing as he made his way along the icy edge of the frozen river.
The picture of a horse treading on ice is the very word for nervousness in Chinese.

What made the horse more nervous still, was an
eye - an eye looking at him from behind a tree on
   the far side of the stream.
Which is to say in Chinese, the eye of a spy. And the
   eye, seeing no one out doors but a horse, stepped out
and showed itself to be a man who tiptoed across
   the frozen river and hurried to the hidden side
of the double-walled storehouse.

門林馬

The horse kept well away at first
"I'm a horse, not a watchdog," he told himself.
   But after a time curiosity pushed him cautiously
forward.
"I suppose I must go and see what he's up to." he thought.

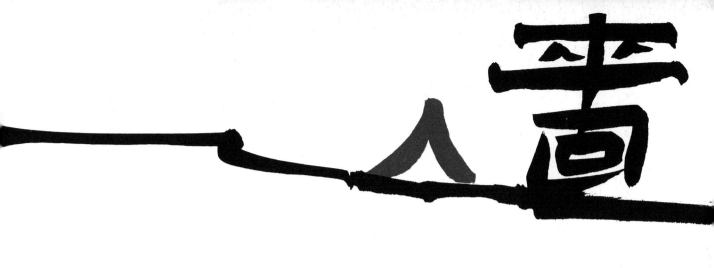

Slowly he nosed his head round to the hidden side of the storehouse. The man was waiting for him.

He rushed at the horse clutching all the grain in two bundles, one under each arm.

Now a man carrying off bundles of stolen grain accuses himself; he is the Chinese word for thief.

The man vaulted on to the horse and dug his heels in his flanks, startling him into a gallop.
The sound of the hooves brought the farmer running out. But he was too late.
All he got was a parting glimpse of the rider.

The thief rode him hard. And when he could gallop him no further, he kept him to a trot, fearing that if they stopped the farmer might still catch up with them.

The horse wondered to himself what he should do. "If I throw him off my back, all that grain will go flying."

He tried slowing down, but the thief's heels spurred him on. And as the sunless day turned greyer, they travelled so far that there was little hope of the farmer catching up.

The thief chewed bits of grain to ease his hunger, but offered none to the horse.

"Does he think," thought the horse, "that before I starve, I'll have carried him as far away as he needs to be?"

And to find out if this were true he said to the man, " If you don't give me a little of that grain, tomorrow morning you'll be going on two legs instead of four. 1 was already half-starved when you made me gallop; a night's ride is all 1 have left in me."

And the thief, thinking that by morning he would have no further use for the horse, answered exactly as the horse had expected," I shall be the judge of when you should be fed!"

He sounded tired as well as angry. And sure enough the horse soon heard the man's breathing slow down with sleepiness.
This gave the horse a very good idea.

As the man dozed off a little, the horse turned a little to one side. And the bundles of grain slipped a little from under the man's relaxing arms, wakening him with a start.

"What are you doing!" he shouted.

"My leg is going limp," the horse said, shrewdly putting a limp in his walk.

After a time the man dozed a little once again, and the horse turned a little, and the grain slipped a little, and the man woke again with a start.

"I'm wide awake," the thief warned him, "so don't try anything." This merely proved to the horse that the man hadn't noticed him turning.

Doze by doze, turn by turn, the horse aimed
the man further and further away from the

direction of escape. The thief nodded off
so often now that the horse could turn more
often, and the grain slipped so often that
the man's eyes were almost fluttering open
and shut.

The sky was clearing and the light of the
sun was showing below the branches of the trees
like the Chinese word for daybreak before dawn.

But the next time the thief felt the grain
slipping, his drooping eyelids leaped wide open.
The farmer's empty storehouse stood right
in front of him. The angry farmer was striding
towards them.

The thief made a fitful move as if to turn the horse round and escape.

"It's no use," the horse said quickly, "I can't gallop with this limp. Instead try this, ask him if anyone has robbed his storehouse."

"But I already know someone has robbed his storehouse," the thief said, stupid from lack of sleep.

"He doesn't know it was you. Tell him you caught someone running away with some grain. Say you are looking for the owner. Ask him," the horse repeated politely, "if anyone has robbed his storehouse."

And, using this story, the thief returned the grain.
But the farmer was not fooled; he had seen the
thief galloping off the day before and remembered
the face.
He made the man a prisoner, a man enclosed
by four walls.

The farmer's wife gave the horse as much of the grain as she could spare, then put the pot on the fire and made porridge. She took a little for herself, and gave a little more to her husband because he would have to go out hunting now to stretch their food supplies, and what was left in the pot she gave to the prisoner.

And perhaps that is why the Chinese word
for charity is a picture of a prisoner with a pot of
hot porridge set down beside him.

CHARITY

Now you know some more Chinese words. If all these stories were told you would know dozens.

THIEF

MAN

FARMER

ICE

PRISONER

COOKING POT

RIVER

DAWN

ROOF

SPY

HORSE

STOREHOUSE

FOREST

WOMAN

NERVOUSNESS

FIRE